FLAWED BUT CALLED

KEVIN L RILEY

We Publish Books, LLC
2213 N Reynolds Rd, Ste 12
Bryant, AR 72022
wepublishbooksllc@gmail.com
501-613-7040

© 2025 Kevin L. Riley. All rights reserved.

No part of this book may be reproduced, stored in a retrieval system, or transmitted by any means without the written permission of the author.

Published by: We Publish Books, LLC

ISBN: 979-8-9927026-06 (Paperback) 3/31/2025

ASIN: B0F1V553FF (eBook) 4/14/2025

Scripture quotations marked KJV are taken from The King James Version present on the Bible Gateway, which matches the 1987 printing. The KJV is public domain in the United States.

The illustrations in this book are graphics used for illustration purposes only and not to depict actual individuals. The graphics are creative works of illustrator, Devin Kittrell.

CONTENTS

Preface 5

Introduction 9

Chapter 1: Moses: Flawed in Speech but Called to Lead 15

Chapter 2: David: Flawed by Sin but Called to be King 27

Chapter 3: Peter: Flawed by Denial but Called to Shepherd 39

Chapter 4: Paul: Flawed by Persecution but Called to Preach 51

Chapter 5: Gideon: Flawed by Fear but Called to Deliver 65

Chapter 6: Jonah: Flawed by Disobedience but Called to Prophesy 75

Chapter 7: Jeremiah: Flawed by Doubt but Called to be a Prophet 87

Closing Remarks 95

PREFACE

In a world where perfection is often idolized, many of us struggle with feelings of inadequacy and self-doubt. We question our worthiness and ability to fulfill the roles we feel called to. Yet, it is within these very struggles that the beauty of God's grace is most evident.

"Flawed but Called" is a testament to the profound truth that God does not call the perfect; He perfects the called. This book invites us to embrace our imperfections as part of God's divine plan. It challenges us to see our weaknesses not as disqualifications but as opportunities for God's strength to shine through.

As you journey through these pages, you will find solace in the lives of biblical figures who God chose for remarkable purposes despite their flaws and failures. Their stories remind us that our imperfections do not negate our potential but affirm our need for God's guidance and grace.

When we begin to view our imperfections as a means for God to demonstrate His glory, our perspective shifts. Our brokenness becomes a vessel for His strength, and our doubts transform into opportunities for His reassurance. Through faith, we discover that our flaws are not liabilities but tools for God to mold us into who we are meant to be.

In "Flawed but Called," you will discover that you are not alone in your struggles. You will be encouraged to shift your focus from your limitations to the boundless possibilities God sees in you. Through this transformative journey, you will learn to view your imperfections as integral to your unique calling and embrace the divine purpose that God has set before you.

May this book inspire you to step boldly into your calling, confident that God's grace is sufficient and that He can use you, just as you are, to accomplish His remarkable work.

Kevin L. Riley

INTRODUCTION

Have you ever thought about whether God can truly use someone like you? This question weighs heavily on the hearts of many people, including myself. We often struggle with our imperfections, making us feel unworthy of participating in ministry or being chosen for His work.

It's easy to become focused on our perceived flaws, those shortcomings we think prevent us from serving effectively. We might believe our mistakes or weaknesses disqualify us from fulfilling a divine purpose. However, amidst that self-doubt, it's important to remember that God sees us not as we see ourselves but as vessels for His grace and love.

In our struggle with feelings of inadequacy, we often overlook an important truth: God has called each of us to fulfill a unique purpose. Embracing this calling requires us to shift our focus from our limitations to the boundless potential that God sees in us. By doing this, we can begin to understand that our imperfections do not diminish our value in His eyes; instead, they remind us of our need for His strength and guidance.

Sadly, many members of the church community develop the belief that their leaders and ministers lead perfectly unblemished lives, free from struggles and flaws. This prevalent misconception creates a set of unrealistic expectations that can weigh heavily on an individual. As a result, those who aspire to serve in ministry may wrestle with feelings of inadequacy, believing they are too imperfect or flawed to fulfill such an honorable calling. This can create a barrier that prevents many from pursuing their desire to contribute meaningfully to their faith community.

FLAWED BUT CALLED

I remember a time when I questioned whether God could use me. Despite my deep and unwavering love for the Lord, I felt flawed. From a young age, I knew I wanted to serve God wholeheartedly and be obedient to His will for my life. However, even with my love for God, I faced various struggles that often contradicted what I believed to be His purpose for me. These struggles included feelings of unworthiness and insecurity stemming from self-esteem issues, which made it increasingly difficult for me to see myself as capable of serving in a meaningful way.

As I delved deeper into the Word of God, I found myself relating more and more to the various individuals He chose to accomplish significant tasks throughout history. During my exploration, I uncovered a remarkable pattern: God often selects people with flaws and imperfections to fulfill His divine purposes. With this realization, I understood that all God required from me was a simple "yes." If I surrendered to His will for my life, "the Lord will perfect that which concerneth me" (Psalm 138:8).

If you have ever wondered whether you are truly worthy of being used by God, let me reassure you: the answer is a resounding yes! You are fully capable of fulfilling His purpose. In the upcoming chapters, I will explore the lives of several significant leaders from the Bible. These individuals, despite their imperfections and challenges, were called by God to achieve remarkable things. Their journeys will demonstrate that it is not our perfection that qualifies us for God's work, but our willingness to respond to His call.

SOMETHING TO PONDER

What imperfections or struggles have made you doubt your ability to be used by God?

CHAPTER 1

Moses: Flawed in Speech but Called to Lead

Scripture Reference: Exodus 4:10-12 (KJV)

And Moses said unto the LORD, O my Lord, I am not eloquent, neither heretofore, nor since thou hast spoken unto thy servant: but I am slow of speech, and of a slow tongue. And the LORD said unto him, Who hath made man's mouth? or who maketh the dumb, or deaf, or the seeing, or the blind? have not I the LORD? Now therefore go, and I will be with thy mouth, and teach thee what thou shalt say.

Few figures are as revered as Moses. His leadership in freeing the Israelites from slavery in Egypt and guiding them toward the Promised Land is one of the Bible's most celebrated stories. This journey, filled with trials, miracles, and divine guidance, showcases his dedication to his people and faith in God.

Despite his achievements, Moses struggled with self-doubt and didn't see himself as a natural leader. He was conscious of his speech impediment, which undermined his confidence and made him feel unprepared. Moses feared this would prevent him from effectively conveying God's messages and commanding the respect needed to lead the diverse Israelites.

Moses' journey was not just about escaping oppression but also about overcoming internal struggles with identity and self-worth. By facing these challenges, he demonstrated that great leaders are often forged through personal obstacles, emerging as symbols of hope and resilience.

The Burden of Inadequacy

Moses' encounter with God at the burning bush is a profoundly transformative moment, filled with deep emotional and spiritual significance. As he stands before the flames that do not consume the bush, Moses feels the weight of his calling. When God commands him to confront Pharaoh and demand the liberation of the Israelites from slavery, Moses responds with genuine vulnerability. He expresses his fears, saying, "O my Lord, I am not eloquent." This statement reveals his anxiety about public speaking and his concern over whether he can effectively convey the important message he has been given.

As he wrestles with his self-doubt, Moses describes himself as having "slow speech" and a "slow tongue," projecting an image of a man painfully aware of his perceived inadequacies. This sincere expression reveals his insecurity and the immense challenge ahead of him, making him feel unworthy and ill-equipped for such a significant mission.

This exchange highlights Moses' deep vulnerability, a sentiment that resonates with many today. It reminds us that feelings of inadequacy often burden those called to a greater purpose. Many worry that their flaws and weaknesses might hinder them from fulfilling their divine calling. Moses' internal struggle reflects the challenges we face when stepping into significant roles, showing that even revered historical figures grappled with doubt and hesitation when confronted with monumental responsibilities.

God's Assurance

God's response to Moses isn't just a statement; it's an empowering affirmation full of reassurance and purpose. In this pivotal moment, God underscores His role as the creator, intimately involved in every aspect of existence, including the design of the human mouth. By asking, "Who has made man's mouth?" God addresses Moses' insecurities and self-doubt about his ability to communicate. This rhetorical question is a powerful reminder of God's supreme authority and infinite power.

God declares with profound clarity, "Have I not, the LORD? Now therefore go, and I will be with your mouth and teach you what you shall say." This promise underscores God's unwavering commitment to guiding and supporting Moses throughout his mission. It reveals an essential truth about God's calling: He doesn't select those already equipped with the necessary talents or skills. Instead, He actively trains and equips those He chooses, ensuring they have everything they need to succeed.

Ultimately, it's not our natural abilities or qualifications that empower us to fulfill God's purpose. Instead, it's His constant presence, support, and guidance that enable us to embrace our roles with confidence. This powerful message inspires believers to respond wholeheartedly to God's call, reassuring them that they can depend on His strength and wisdom to navigate their paths and realize their destinies even in the face of fears or feelings of inadequacy.

Embracing Our Weaknesses

Moses' story illustrates how our perceived weaknesses can showcase God's extraordinary strength. Initially, Moses was filled with hesitation and self-doubt, feeling inadequate for the monumental task of freeing the Israelites from slavery; however, he ultimately embraced God's call, setting into motion a series of awe-inspiring events that defined his life.

With unwavering determination, Moses confronted Pharaoh, demanding the release of the enslaved Israelites. This act was a profound testament to his faith and commitment to his people and to God. Guided by divine wisdom, Moses led the Israelites through the parted Red Sea—a miracle that enabled them to escape their oppressors and begin their journey to freedom.

Moreover, on Mount Sinai, Moses received the Ten Commandments, providing the Israelites with a foundational moral code. These achievements were not due to Moses' perfection, but his profound trust in God's promise to be with him every step of the way. Moses' story underscores the truth that when we embrace our vulnerabilities and turn to our faith, we can accomplish extraordinary feats that reflect the strength of the divine.

The Power of Divine Support

Moses' story is a powerful reminder that our flaws and imperfections are not barriers to God's purpose. Instead, these shortcomings can become gateways for His divine power to manifest in our lives. When we confront our limitations and trust in God's strength, we invite His transformative work in ways we never imagined.

Moses' journey is particularly inspiring. He began burdened by self-doubt and insecurity, feeling inadequate. Yet, through profound encounters with God and a commitment to his calling, he evolved into a courageous leader. This transformation empowered him to guide the Israelites out of slavery in Egypt, marking a significant turning point in their history.

Moses' life shows how divine support can lead to profound personal growth and help us realize our potential. His story encourages us to see our vulnerabilities as sources of strength. It reassures us that we are never alone in our endeavors. By embracing our flaws, we open ourselves to making a significant impact in the world around us.

A Call to Action

Reflecting on Moses' story, we're reminded of the importance of embracing our imperfections. We all face moments of inadequacy or doubt about our worthiness to answer God's call. However, God's invitation to serve doesn't depend on our abilities or past achievements. He sees the potential within us, even when we focus on our limitations. God's promise is to accompany us on our journey, providing guidance, strength, and empowerment every step of the way.

As we explore the lives of other notable biblical figures, we'll see how, like Moses, they were imperfect yet chosen by God to achieve remarkable feats. Their stories offer profound lessons that resonate with our own journeys, showing that perfection isn't necessary for divine purpose. It is our openness to God's call and trust in His provision and grace that truly qualifies us for the work He sets before us. By examining these stories, we'll understand how God can turn our flaws into strengths, helping us fulfill purposes that transcend our individual lives and contribute to His greater plan.

SOMETHING TO PONDER

What personal weaknesses have you struggled with, and how can you trust in God's strength to overcome them?

CHAPTER 2

David: Flawed by Sin but Called to be King

Scripture Reference: 2 Samuel 12:13-14 (KJV)

And David said unto Nathan, I have sinned against the LORD. And Nathan said unto David, The LORD also hath put away thy sin; thou shalt not die. Howbeit, because by this deed thou hast given great occasion to the enemies of the LORD to blaspheme, the child also that is born unto thee shall surely die.

David, known as a man after God's own heart, is a prominent figure in biblical history. His life offers profound lessons through his multifaceted character, showcasing both deep faith and significant moral failures.

From his humble beginnings as a shepherd to his rise as King of Israel, David's journey is filled with triumphs and tragedies. He is celebrated for his unwavering faith, seen in his victory over Goliath and his heartfelt psalms. However, his story also includes severe lapses in judgment, such as his adultery with Bathsheba and the arranged death of her husband, Uriah.

These failings do not negate David's status or calling. Instead, they highlight his ability to sincerely repent and seek God's forgiveness. David's life underscores the truth that God's call remains intact despite our imperfections. We learn that repentance, grace, and forgiveness are vital in our relationship with

God and that deep faith can coexist with our struggles and failures.

The Weight of Sin

David's sin with Bathsheba stands out as one of his life's most well-known and distressing narratives. The story begins when David, gazing from the rooftop of his palace, sees Bathsheba bathing. She is the wife of Uriah, a loyal soldier serving in David's army. Unable to resist his desire, David summons Bathsheba and engages in an adulterous affair with her. When Bathsheba later informs him that she is pregnant, David, desperate to conceal his wrongdoing, devises a plan that ultimately leads to Uriah's death on the battlefield.

To carry out this scheme, David orders that Uriah be placed at the front lines of the fiercest fighting, ensuring that he would be killed. This heinous act marks a significant moral decline for David, resulting in severe consequences for him personally and for the nation of Israel as a whole. The repercussions of his actions reverberate through his family and court, leading to turmoil and strife.

The turning point in this dark chapter comes when the prophet Nathan confronts David. Nathan tells a captivating parable about a rich man who ruthlessly takes the only lamb of a poor man to feed a traveler, evoking David's anger. When Nathan reveals that the rich man symbolizes David himself, David is struck by the weight of his sin. This moment of confrontation leads him to acknowledge his transgressions, and he offers a heartfelt confession, exclaiming, "I have sinned against the LORD." This realization marks a profound awakening for David, filled with deep remorse for his actions and a recognition of the consequences that would follow.

God's Grace and Forgiveness

Nathan's response to David's confession powerfully illustrates the profound nature of God's grace. He communicates to David, "The LORD has also put away your sin; you shall not die." This statement reveals that, despite the gravity of David's transgressions—including adultery and murder—God's willingness to forgive him remains true. Nathan's words signify that David's life would be spared, a testament to God's mercy.

However, Nathan also makes it clear that while God's forgiveness is complete, the consequences of David's actions would still unfold. He solemnly warns David that his misdeeds have provided those who oppose the LORD with an opportunity to mock and blaspheme. Due to this, Nathan informs David that the child born to him and Bathsheba would not survive. This agonizing moment underscores the reality that even after forgiveness, the repercussions of our choices can be far-reaching and painful.

This duality in God's response—granting forgiveness while allowing consequences to persist—reveals an important truth about divine grace. It emphasizes that while God's mercy is unfathomable and can restore our standing with Him, it does not shield us from the outcomes of our actions. David's narrative serves as a powerful reminder that true repentance is essential to rekindle our relationship with God, providing us with a path toward healing and restoration. However, it also calls us to acknowledge that our decisions have lasting effects that we must confront, underscoring the complexity of grace in the face of human fallibility.

A Heart of Repentance

David's journey of repentance is profoundly articulated in Psalm 51, a heartfelt expression of his desire for mercy and spiritual renewal. In this emotional psalm, David implores, "Create in me a clean heart, O God; and renew a right spirit within me." This powerful plea encapsulates the core of genuine repentance: a sincere intent to turn away from sin and a deep yearning for restoration in one's relationship with God.

What makes David's repentance particularly compelling is his openness in confronting his wrongdoings. He does not shy away from acknowledging his sins, which serves as a crucial example for all believers. It underscores a vital truth: no matter how deeply one may fall into sin, God's grace is always available to offer forgiveness and redemption. David illustrates that repentance involves more than merely asking for pardon; it requires a transformative process of realigning one's life with God's will and purpose.

His heartfelt reflection in Psalm 51 reveals an understanding that true repentance also necessitates a change of heart and mind—a commitment to not only seek forgiveness but to strive to live in accordance with God's commands. David's earnest quest for a renewed spirit highlights the importance of humility and the acknowledgment of our need for divine intervention. Through his example, believers are reminded that every moment is an opportunity for restoration, reinforcing the boundless love and grace that God extends to those who earnestly seek Him.

The Restoration of a King

Despite his numerous flaws and failures, David continued to be recognized as God's chosen king of Israel. His kingship stands as a powerful testament to the belief that God's call is irrevocable and unwavering. Throughout David's reign, he experienced a remarkable blend of triumph and tragedy. He achieved great military victories and united the nation, yet he also faced profound personal failures and hardships. Nevertheless, through all these challenges, he remained a man after God's own heart, illustrating resilience in his relationship with God.

David's life serves as a compelling reminder that our failures and shortcomings do not disqualify us from fulfilling the purpose God has for us. His story emphasizes that God's choice is not contingent on our past mistakes or moral standing; rather, God's selection of David as king, despite his sinful actions, highlights the profound truth that His call is rooted in grace rather than our merit or righteousness.

This reality invites every believer to fully embrace the depth of God's forgiveness and mercy. It encourages us to move forward confidently into the roles and responsibilities He has designed for us, reassuring us that we are not defined by our past but rather by the grace and calling of God in our lives. Through David's example, we find hope and inspiration to pursue our God-given destinies, regardless of the mistakes we've made along the way.

Embracing God's Call

As we take time to reflect on the story of David, we are reminded of the importance of embracing God's call in our lives, even when we recognize our imperfections. David, a man after God's own heart, faced numerous challenges and moments of profound failure throughout his life. These experiences serve as a powerful reminder that despite our shortcomings, God's grace is abundantly sufficient to bring us back to a place of restoration.

FLAWED BUT CALLED

When we confront our own failures, it is through genuine repentance that we find the pathway to His forgiveness. This act of turning back to God allows us to shed the weight of our mistakes and encourages us to step forward with renewed purpose. Just as David was able to continue fulfilling God's plan despite his missteps, we too can move ahead with confidence, knowing that God's love and mercy will guide us. Let us remember that our journey is not defined by our failures but by our willingness to seek God and align ourselves with His will.

CHAPTER 3

Peter: Flawed by Denial but Called to Shepherd

Scripture Reference: John 21:15-17 (KJV)

So when they had dined, Jesus saith to Simon Peter, Simon, son of Jonas, lovest thou me more than these? He saith unto him, Yea, Lord; thou knowest that I love thee. He saith unto him, Feed my lambs. He saith to him again the second time, Simon, son of Jonas, lovest thou me? He saith unto him, Yea, Lord; thou knowest that I love thee. He saith unto him, Feed my sheep. He saith unto him the third time, Simon, son of Jonas, lovest thou me? Peter was grieved because he said unto him the third time, Lovest thou me? And he said unto him, Lord, thou knowest all things; thou knowest that I love thee. Jesus saith unto him, Feed my sheep.

Peter stands out among the disciples for his extraordinary courage, unwavering loyalty, and profound humanity. His journey is a mix of triumphs and struggles, reflecting the complexities of a life of faith. One of the most pivotal moments in Peter's story is his denial of Jesus, a heartbreaking act that reveals his human frailty and fear. However, this failure is followed by a powerful restoration when Jesus forgives and reinstates him, commissioning Peter to shepherd and guide His followers. This transformation highlights the theme of redemption and underscores Peter's crucial role in the early Church as a devoted leader committed to nurturing and strengthening the faith of others.

The Agony of Denial

On the night Jesus was arrested, Peter faced a test of his faith and resolve. Driven by fear for his safety amid the chaos, he denied knowing Jesus three times. This was especially striking because it sharply contrasted with Peter's earlier assertions of loyalty, where he had boldly proclaimed he would never abandon Jesus, even in danger.

With each denial, Peter felt a growing sense of dread and guilt. When the rooster crowed, fulfilling Jesus' earlier prophecy, Peter was overwhelmed by remorse. The weight of his actions hit him hard, reminding him of his vulnerability and the complexity of human nature.

Peter's experience shows how fear can challenge our convictions. Even those with strong beliefs can falter under pressure and betray what they hold dear.

His story serves as a stirring lesson about the challenges of maintaining integrity when faced with anxiety and societal pressures.

The Path to Restoration

Following His resurrection, Jesus made several meaningful appearances to His disciples. One of the most impactful took place on the shores of the Sea of Galilee, a familiar spot for the disciples, where they had spent countless hours fishing and learning from Jesus.

During this moment, Jesus focused on Peter, who was struggling with guilt and remorse after denying Jesus three times before the crucifixion. Instead of confronting Peter with blame or anger, Jesus offered a path to healing and reconciliation. He asked Peter three times, "Simon, son of Jonas, do you love me?" This mirrored Peter's earlier denials and served as a powerful reminder of Jesus' grace and forgiveness.

Each question gave Peter a chance to reflect on his love and commitment to Jesus. With each affirmation, Peter not only restored his relationship with Jesus but also reaffirmed his role within the community of disciples. This exchange highlights the themes of redemption and unwavering love, showcasing Jesus' intent to heal wounds and empower His followers to move forward in faith.

A Commission to Shepherd

Jesus' repeated question, "Do you love me?" went deeper than just gauging Peter's emotions; it was an invitation for Peter to rediscover his purpose and commitment. Each time Peter affirmed his love, Jesus responded with a specific task: "Feed my lambs" and "Feed my sheep." By saying this, Jesus was giving Peter the responsibility to care for His followers, effectively appointing him as a shepherd to guide and nurture the community of believers.

This moment was especially significant because of Peter's earlier denials of Jesus. Despite his failures, Jesus restored him to a position of leadership and trust. This act showed that past mistakes don't disqualify anyone from a future filled with purpose. Instead, it highlighted the power of grace and the ongoing opportunity for redemption. Jesus' commissioning of Peter emphasized that love and commitment can lead to new beginnings, no matter past shortcomings. Through this conversation, Jesus gave Peter—and all believers—a message of hope and renewal, inviting them to experience a restored sense of purpose.

FLAWED BUT CALLED

Embracing Forgiveness and Purpose

Peter's restoration is a powerful example of God's grace and forgiveness in action. It shows that our mistakes and shortcomings don't make us unworthy of serving God. In fact, these failures can become the moments where God's power and purpose shine the brightest.

Peter's journey is especially striking. He went from denying Jesus during the turmoil of the crucifixion to becoming a key leader in the early Church. This transformation highlights that God's call is rooted in His unwavering love and mercy, not in our perfection. Rather than being cast aside, Peter was invited into a deeper relationship and responsibility, demonstrating that redemption is always possible and that everyone has a role in God's plan, regardless of their past.

A Reflection for Today

Peter's story reminds us that our personal flaws and moments of weakness don't disqualify us from serving God. Like Peter, who faced many challenges and failures, we may also stumble in our lives. However, God's call on our lives remains steadfast and unwavering, regardless of our past mistakes.

God's forgiveness is not just a superficial acknowledgment of our shortcomings; it provides a profound path to restoration. No matter how many times we falter, we have the opportunity to be renewed and step into the roles He has prepared for us. Each of us has a purpose in God's plan, and His grace empowers us to fulfill it, even after we have erred.

Peter's experience encourages us to embrace God's forgiveness and seek His guidance as we navigate our lives and strive to fulfill our calling. It reminds us that our identity in Christ is defined not by our failures but by His unwavering love, grace, and acceptance. Through Him, we can move forward with confidence and purpose, knowing we are cherished and valued in His eyes.

Moving Forward in Faith

Let Peter's journey inspire you to fully embrace the grace that God offers. Like Peter, you may experience moments of failure and struggle, but you can rise above your own shortcomings. Remember, God has placed a unique calling on your life, tailored to you and your experiences.

By accepting this call, you will discover the remarkable ways in which God wants to work through you. You are equipped with the qualities and gifts needed to make a difference in the world around you. As you step into this calling, you will have the opportunity to guide and positively influence others in ways you may not have imagined. Embrace the journey and watch how God transforms your life and the lives of those you touch.

SOMETHING TO PONDER

Think of a time when you denied your faith. How did you seek forgiveness and restore your relationship with God?

CHAPTER 4

Paul: Flawed by Persecution but Called to Preach

Scripture Reference: Acts 9:15-16 (KJV)

But the Lord said unto him, Go thy way: for he is a chosen vessel unto me, to bear my name before the Gentiles, and kings, and the children of Israel: For I will shew him how great things he must suffer for my name's sake.

Paul, originally known as Saul of Tarsus, is one of the most significant figures in the New Testament. His life story is a compelling narrative of transformation, showing the profound change that can come from a divine calling. Initially, Paul fervently opposed the early Christian movement, actively persecuting believers and seeking to suppress their teachings. His zeal for his beliefs led him to imprison many Christians and even approve their executions.

However, everything changed during a dramatic encounter on the road to Damascus. While traveling to arrest more Christians, Paul experienced a blinding light and heard the voice of Jesus asking, "Saul, why are you persecuting me?" This pivotal moment marked the beginning of his conversion. After this experience, he dedicated himself to understanding the message of Christ, eventually becoming one of Christianity's most passionate advocates.

Paul's mission extended beyond the Jewish community, as he felt called to preach the gospel to the Gentiles. His extensive travels throughout the Roman Empire allowed him to establish numerous churches and spread Christian teachings far and wide. He authored several letters, now part of the New Testament, that continue to influence Christian theology and practice today. Paul's remarkable journey shows the incredible potential for redemption and the impact of God's grace in transforming lives for a greater purpose.

The Persecutor

Before his dramatic conversion, Saul of Tarsus was known for his intense persecution of early Christians. As a devout Pharisee, he believed he was defending the Jewish faith against what he saw as a dangerous sect. Saul aggressively sought out followers of Jesus, raiding their gatherings and imprisoning them. He even approved the execution of Christians, thinking he was protecting his religious beliefs. His relentless actions instilled fear in many believers, causing widespread suffering. Saul became one of the most formidable adversaries of the early Church, creating significant obstacles for the spread of Christianity.

The Damascus Road Encounter

Saul's life took a dramatic turn while traveling on the road to Damascus, intending to arrest Christians. Suddenly, a blinding light from heaven enveloped him, causing him to fall in shock. He heard a voice asking, "Saul, Saul, why are you persecuting me?" This encounter with the risen Christ left Saul momentarily blind and deeply shaken, prompting him to question his beliefs and actions.

After this event, the Lord reached out to Ananias, a disciple in Damascus. God instructed Ananias to find

Saul and restore his sight. Although hesitant due to Saul's reputation as a persecutor, Ananias obeyed.

Meeting Saul in a house on Straight Street, Ananias compassionately laid his hands on him and said, "Brother Saul, the Lord Jesus, who appeared to you on the road, has sent me so you may regain your sight and be filled with the Holy Spirit." Instantly, something like scales fell from Saul's eyes, and his sight was restored. This marked the pivotal beginning of Saul's transformation into Paul, the apostle, who would spread Christianity worldwide. This encounter changed his life forever, turning him from a persecutor into one of the faith's most influential advocates.

A Chosen Vessel

God's message to Ananias was clear and profound: "Go your way, for he is a chosen vessel unto me, to bear my name before the Gentiles, kings, and the children of Israel." This emphasizes God's intention to use Saul, despite his past of persecuting Christians, as a key figure in spreading the Gospel. God saw beyond Saul's violent history and recognized his potential for a greater purpose.

Saul, later known as Paul, becoming an apostle shows a fundamental truth about divine grace: no one is beyond God's call and redemption. This story reminds us that God's grace can not only forgive but also transform even the most flawed individuals. By redeeming Saul and appointing him to carry Christ's message to both Jews and Gentiles, God demonstrated that He can use anyone to fulfill His plan, turning former enemies into ambassadors of love and truth to advance His kingdom.

Embracing the Call

Paul's conversion was a transformative event with significant challenges. After his dramatic encounter with Christ on the road to Damascus, he faced deep suspicion and hostility from those who remembered him as a persecutor of Christians. Many were understandably reluctant to accept him, fearing his conversion might be a deceptive act to undermine their faith.

Despite these obstacles, Paul's commitment to his newfound faith was unwavering. He passionately embraced the gospel message and began his ministry in Damascus, boldly proclaiming Jesus. His efforts quickly attracted attention, leading to both conversions and opposition.

As time went on, Paul's mission expanded. He traveled extensively throughout the Roman Empire, establishing churches in major cities and regions. His ministry was marked by immense dedication, often facing imprisonment, beatings, and threats to his life—all for the sake of sharing the gospel.

In addition to his commitment, Paul's teachings reflected profound theological insights. He emphasized themes like grace, redemption, and the significance of Christ's resurrection. His writings, many of which became books of the New Testament, continue to influence Christian thought today.

Ultimately, Paul's willingness to suffer for his beliefs became a hallmark of his ministry. He endured numerous trials, viewing them as a testament to his faith and the importance of spreading Christ's message. His journey from persecutor to passionate preacher exemplifies the transformative power of faith and the challenges that often accompany such profound change.

The Cost of Discipleship

God's message to Ananias included a profound and sobering prophecy: "For I will show him how great things he must suffer for my name's sake." This message foreshadowed the challenging journey that the Apostle Paul would undertake. Throughout his life and ministry, Paul encountered a multitude of hardships that tested his faith and resolve. He suffered imprisonment on multiple occasions, faced brutal beatings at the hands of his opponents, endured shipwrecks that left him stranded and in peril, and encountered countless other trials that would have discouraged many.

Despite these overwhelming challenges, Paul remained unwavering in his commitment to his mission of preaching Christ and spreading the gospel message. His determination and resilience serve as a powerful testimony to the cost of true discipleship. Paul's life exemplifies the notion that answering God's call often requires significant sacrifice, relentless perseverance, and an unyielding spirit in the face of adversity.

Moreover, while the path of discipleship is fraught with difficulties, it is also enriched with profound fulfillment. Paul experienced the joy and purpose that come from serving a cause greater than oneself. His example encourages believers today to persevere through their own struggles, knowing that the work they do in service of God can yield remarkable spiritual rewards and transformation.

A Legacy of Faith

Paul's influence on the early Church and Christian theology is immense. His letters, known as epistles, were addressed to various Christian communities across the Roman Empire and make up a significant part of the New Testament. These writings not only articulate key theological concepts but also address practical issues of faith and community life, offering timeless guidance and inspiration to believers.

Paul's journey is particularly remarkable. Once known as Saul of Tarsus, he was a zealous persecutor of Christians. However, after a dramatic encounter with Christ on the road to Damascus, he underwent a profound transformation. This pivotal moment marked the beginning of his life as a devoted apostle, spreading the message of Jesus and establishing churches.

His writings reveal deep theological insights, including grace, redemption, and the nature of the Church. Despite his flawed past, Paul became a significant figure in early Christianity, showing how God's grace can profoundly change a person's life. His unwavering commitment to his mission and his ability to communicate complex spiritual truths continue to inspire and guide Christians, showcasing his lasting legacy.

Embracing Our Own Call

As we reflect on Paul's journey, let's find encouragement to embrace God's call in our own lives. We all have a history filled with mistakes and imperfections, but God's grace is powerful enough to redeem us and bring about profound transformation. Just as Paul, who once persecuted Christians, became one of the most influential apostles, we too can be changed in remarkable ways.

Through God's mercy, we can become vessels of His love and truth, sharing His message with the world. Our past does not define us; it can instead serve as a testament to the power of grace and redemption. Let's open our hearts and allow God's transformative work to guide us as we carry His name and mission to those around us.

SOMETHING TO PONDER

Think of a major change in your life. How did it affect your faith and purpose?

CHAPTER 5

Gideon: Flawed by Fear but Called to Deliver

Scripture Reference: Judges 6:15-16 (KJV)

And he said unto him, Oh my Lord, wherewith shall I save Israel? behold, my family is poor in Manasseh, and I am the least in my father's house. And the LORD said unto him, Surely I will be with thee, and thou shalt smite the Midianites as one man.

Gideon is an unexpected hero, showing that God often calls those who feel the least equipped to fulfill His grand purposes. Initially, Gideon was filled with fear and self-doubt, thinking he lacked the strength and skills needed to lead the Israelites against their oppressors. Despite his reservations, God saw potential in him and provided the reassurance he needed.

As Gideon embarked on his journey, he transformed from a hesitant individual into a courageous warrior, becoming a mighty deliverer for Israel. This remarkable change highlights the powerful impact of God's presence in one's life—instilling courage, confidence, and the ability to overcome seemingly insurmountable challenges. Gideon's story reminds us that even those who feel inadequate can be used by God to achieve significant and far-reaching purposes.

FLAWED BUT CALLED

The Weight of Fear and Inadequacy

When the angel of the LORD appeared to Gideon, he found him hiding in a winepress, secretly threshing wheat to avoid the Midianites who were oppressing the Israelites. Seeing Gideon laboring in fear, the angel greeted him powerfully: "The LORD is with you, mighty warrior."

Gideon's immediate reaction showed his deep sense of inadequacy and disbelief. He replied, "Oh my Lord, how can I save Israel? My family is the weakest in the tribe of Manasseh, and I am the least in my father's house." This response highlighted his feelings of inferiority and the desperate circumstances of his clan, emphasizing his perceived unworthiness for such a monumental task.

Despite Gideon's fears and the overwhelming odds against him, this moment marked the beginning of his journey as a leader. He was called to rise above his limitations and lead his people to victory, showing that God often chooses those who feel insignificant to achieve great things.

God's Assurance

God's response to Gideon's fears was immediate and profound. He reassured Gideon by saying, "I will be with you, and you will defeat the Midianites as if they were just one man." This promise was significant, not because of Gideon's abilities or status, but because it was grounded in God's unwavering presence and power.

This reassurance reminds us that our personal limitations—whether they be talents, resources, or confidence—do not restrict God's ability to work through us. When He calls us to fulfill a purpose or take on a challenge, He also provides the necessary strength, wisdom, and guidance to succeed. Through God's empowerment, we can accomplish tasks and overcome obstacles that may seem impossible, fostering hope and courage in the face of adversity.

Testing and Confirming the Call

Despite God's assurance, Gideon felt overwhelmed by the task ahead. Seeking further confirmation, he asked for tangible signs to strengthen his faith. One notable test involved a fleece: Gideon asked God to make the fleece wet with dew while keeping the surrounding ground dry. When God fulfilled this request, Gideon, still uncertain, asked for a reverse sign—this time requesting that the fleece remain dry while the ground was covered with dew.

God graciously and patiently provided the signs Gideon sought, reaffirming His promise and understanding Gideon's doubts and fears. This interaction highlights an important element of Gideon's journey: the need for God's confirmation and assurance. It serves as a reminder that even great leaders can experience uncertainty. Faith often requires courage and support, especially when facing daunting tasks. Gideon's story encourages us to openly communicate our doubts and seek guidance, validating the need for divine reassurance in following God's call.

The Victory Over the Midianites

With God's assurance guiding him, Gideon assembled a small army to confront the powerful Midianites, who had been oppressing the Israelites. Although he initially gathered a larger force, God instructed Gideon to reduce his troops, leaving him with only 300 men. This reduction emphasized that the victory would come from God's power, not human strength or numbers.

FLAWED BUT CALLED

Armed with unconventional weapons—trumpets, pitchers, and torches—Gideon devised a bold nighttime surprise attack. His men surrounded the Midianite camp and, on his signal, shattered their pitchers, revealed their torches, and sounded their trumpets. The overwhelming noise and light caused confusion and panic among the Midianites, leading them to turn on each other and ultimately be defeated.

This miraculous triumph, achieved with such unconventional tactics, highlights a powerful theme: that God's call is always accompanied by His presence and strength. Gideon's story reminds us that even when we feel fearful and weak, God's power can bring about extraordinary outcomes, turning seemingly impossible situations into remarkable victories.

A Reflection for Today

Gideon's journey from fear to faith is a story that resonates deeply with believers. It shows that God doesn't choose us based on our skills, accomplishments, or social status, but according to His divine plan, emphasizing the importance of our willingness to respond to His call.

Throughout Gideon's experiences, we see how feelings of inadequacy and fear can cloud our judgment and hold us back. However, God meets these insecurities with unwavering assurance, promising His constant presence and support. This divine companionship empowers us to rise above our fears and embrace the unique callings placed on our lives.

Gideon's story invites us to trust in God's presence and strength. Our perceived limitations, whether they come from a lack of experience, confidence, or resources, do not stop God from working through us. These limitations can actually highlight God's power, showing that His strength is made perfect in our weakness.

Gideon's eventual victory over seemingly insurmountable odds serves as a testament to the effectiveness of faith coupled with obedience. It reassures us that when God calls us to a task, He also equips us with the necessary tools and abilities to succeed. Moreover, His presence means we are not facing challenges alone; we have the support of an all-powerful God by our side, guiding and empowering us. This truth encourages us to step out in faith, knowing that our journey, no matter how daunting, is part of a divine purpose that will ultimately lead to triumph.

CHAPTER 6

Jonah: Flawed by Disobedience but Called to Prophesy

Scripture Reference: Jonah 1:1-3 (KJV)

Now the word of the LORD came unto Jonah the son of Amittai, saying, Arise, go to Nineveh, that great city, and cry against it; for their wickedness is come up before me. But Jonah rose up to flee unto Tarshish from the presence of the LORD, and went down to Joppa; and he found a ship going to Tarshish: so he paid the fare thereof, and went down into it, to go with them unto Tarshish from the presence of the LORD.

Jonah, a prophet chosen by God, is best known for trying to run away from his divine mission. His story highlights the struggle between human reluctance and God's unwavering persistence. Initially, Jonah tried to escape his responsibility by boarding a ship to Tarshish, moving in the opposite direction from Nineveh, where God had commanded him to preach repentance. This act of disobedience led to dramatic events, including a fierce storm and Jonah being swallowed by a great fish.

Inside the fish, Jonah experienced a transformation, reflecting on his actions and his relationship with God. His prayer of repentance prompted the fish to release him back onto dry land. Eventually, Jonah carried out his mission in Nineveh, where his message led the people to repent and turn back to God. This journey highlights Jonah's initial reluctance but also reveals God's immense mercy and compassion, showing that even those who stray can find redemption when they heed His call.

The Flight from God's Command

God's instruction to Jonah was unmistakably clear: "Arise, go to Nineveh, that great city, and cry against it, for their wickedness has come up before me." Nineveh, the capital of the ancient Assyrian Empire, was infamous for its moral depravity and cruelty. Its people were known for their violent actions and blatant disregard for justice, which drew God's concern.

Instead of obeying, Jonah decided to flee in the opposite direction by boarding a ship to Tarshish, a far-off trading city. This act of disobedience was more than just an escape; it was Jonah's attempt to avoid what he saw as an overwhelming mission. His choice reflected a deep-seated fear of the unknown and possibly a prejudice against the people of Nineveh, whom he may have thought undeserving of mercy. Additionally, he might have doubted the effectiveness of God's plan or worried about how the people of Nineveh would react to his warning.

Jonah's flight represents a common human tendency to avoid uncomfortable tasks or moral dilemmas. His hesitation to go to Nineveh highlights not just his personal struggles, but also the broader conflict many of us face between our own desires and the call of a higher purpose. This internal struggle reminds us that the path of obedience is often filled with challenges that test our faith and resolve.

The Consequences of Disobedience

Jonah's attempt to escape from God's call set off a dramatic chain of events. He boarded a ship to Tarshish, hoping to get away, but a furious storm suddenly erupted, violently tossing the vessel and endangering everyone on board. The terrified sailors prayed to their gods for deliverance while struggling to keep the ship afloat.

Amid the chaos, Jonah realized his disobedience was the cause of the storm. Taking responsibility, he told the sailors to throw him overboard, believing it would calm the sea and save their lives. Reluctantly, they complied, and as Jonah plunged into the water, the storm ceased immediately, leaving an eerie calm.

In that moment, Jonah was swallowed by a great fish, an act both terrifying and miraculous. Inside the fish's belly, he was engulfed in solitude and reflection. For three days and nights, Jonah faced his guilt, fear, and sense of failure. During this time, he prayed, expressing his anguish and repentance to God.

Jonah acknowledged God's sovereignty and mercy, realizing he had turned away from His will. This period of introspection and spiritual awakening was pivotal in Jonah's journey, leading him to a renewed commitment to fulfill his divine mission and share the message of repentance with the people of Nineveh.

God's Persistent Call

After Jonah was released from the belly of the fish, he received a renewed command from God: "Go to Nineveh and proclaim the message I have given you." Despite his initial fear and reluctance, Jonah finally decided to obey.

When he arrived in Nineveh, a city known for its wealth and wickedness, Jonah boldly declared, "In just forty days, Nineveh will be overthrown." His proclamation echoed through the streets, capturing the attention of the city's residents.

FLAWED BUT CALLED

To Jonah's surprise, the response was immediate and overwhelming. From the highest-ranking officials to the poorest citizens, everyone took Jonah's warning seriously. They called for a fast, rejecting food and drink, and adorned themselves in sackcloth—a symbol of mourning and penitence. Even the king of Nineveh joined in, urging everyone, including animals, to participate in the fast, reflecting a profound collective remorse.

As the days passed, the people turned away from their wicked ways, seeking forgiveness and showing a genuine desire to change. God observed their sincere repentance and chose to relent from the calamity He had threatened.

Jonah's hesitant obedience led to one of the most remarkable instances of mass repentance in biblical history, showcasing the power of a simple message when met with genuine humility and contrition.

The Lesson of Jonah

Jonah's story provides valuable insights into divine calling and human response. It shows that our disobedience doesn't negate God's call on our lives. Even though Jonah tried to flee from God's instructions, this didn't disqualify him from being an instrument of God's will. Jonah's journey illustrates that God's purposes can still be accomplished despite our flaws and failures. His call is unwavering and persistent, demonstrating His boundless mercy.

Moreover, Jonah's narrative emphasizes the importance of obeying God's commands and the ripple effect our choices can have on the world around us. After resisting God's directive, Jonah eventually complied, leading to the repentance and salvation of an entire city, Nineveh. This transformation shows that our actions in alignment with God's will can have remarkable and far-reaching outcomes. It reminds us that while we may plan our own paths, God's plans are infinitely greater. Our willingness to surrender and follow His direction can bring about extraordinary changes in our lives and the lives of others.

A Reflection for Today

As we dive into Jonah's story, we're reminded of God's unwavering call, which stays strong even when we try to avoid it. Jonah's narrative shows that our imperfections and acts of disobedience don't stop God's ultimate purposes. Instead, they become chances for His mercy and power to shine in our lives.

Jonah's journey encourages us to embrace God's call with obedience and trust. His experiences highlight the importance of responding positively to divine direction, even when it's tough. This story reassures us that, despite our mistakes and failures, God's grace is more than enough to restore us and realign us with His path.

Additionally, Jonah's transformation from reluctance to obedience emphasizes the crucial role we play in responding to God's invitations. Our responsibility is to be open to His call, allowing Him to guide us and trusting that His plans are filled with purpose. By doing so, we open ourselves to witnessing His great works unfold through our lives, contributing to a greater story of redemption and grace.

SOMETHING TO PONDER

Have you ever tried to avoid an assignment from God? What was the outcome?

CHAPTER 7

Jeremiah: Flawed by Doubt but Called to be a Prophet

Scripture Reference: Jeremiah 1:6-8 (KJV)

Then said I, Ah, Lord GOD! behold, I cannot speak: for I am a child. But the LORD said unto me, Say not, I am a child: for thou shalt go to all that I shall send thee, and whatsoever I command thee thou shalt speak. Be not afraid of their faces: for I am with thee to deliver thee, saith the LORD.

Jeremiah, often called the "weeping prophet," is a great example of someone who faced deep doubt and intense feelings of inadequacy. Despite these struggles, he was chosen by God to deliver an important message to the nations—a task requiring immense courage and conviction. Jeremiah's journey shows us a powerful truth: our doubts and insecurities don't undermine God's call on our lives. Instead, they highlight our need for divine support. Throughout his ministry, Jeremiah experienced God's unwavering presence, which gave him the assurance, strength, and guidance needed to carry out his mission. His story reminds us that we can fulfill our purpose, even when we feel inadequate.

The Weight of Doubt

When God called Jeremiah to be His prophet, Jeremiah's first reaction was filled with doubt and reluctance. He said, "Ah, Lord GOD! Behold, I cannot speak, for I am a child," showing his deep feelings of inadequacy and belief that his youth made him unfit for such an important role. This reaction not only illustrates Jeremiah's personal struggles but also highlights a common human tendency: focusing on our limitations instead of recognizing and embracing God's empowering presence in our lives.

Jeremiah was keenly aware of the challenges ahead. He knew the magnitude of the task God was giving him—to deliver difficult messages to the people of Israel, a responsibility he felt unprepared for. His self-doubt mirrors the feelings many of us experience when faced with big challenges or when we feel called to a divine purpose. Like Jeremiah, we often see ourselves as insufficient or unworthy, forgetting that it is not our own strength that qualifies us, but rather God's guidance and power that equip us for the journey ahead. This theme of empowerment and overcoming personal obstacles runs through many biblical stories, reminding us that we are not alone in our struggles.

God's Reassurance

God's response to Jeremiah's doubts was direct and filled with reassurance. He said, "Do not say, 'I am a child,' for you will go to everyone I send you to, and whatever I command you, you will speak." This statement from God was meant to extinguish Jeremiah's feelings of inadequacy and hesitation, emphasizing that his youth and inexperience should not stop him from fulfilling his divine calling.

God's message was clear: Jeremiah was chosen for an important role that required courage and obedience. He was instructed to travel far and wide to deliver the messages God would provide. The success of Jeremiah's mission depended not on his personal skills or confidence but on God's authority and guidance. This assurance was meant to empower Jeremiah, encouraging him to trust in a higher power that would equip him for the tasks ahead, regardless of his perceived limitations.

The Promise of Presence

God's reassurance to Jeremiah went beyond just issuing a command; it came with a profound promise. The Lord said, "Do not be afraid of them, for I am with you to deliver you." This declaration emphasized not only God's presence but also His commitment to protect and rescue Jeremiah from the challenges ahead.

This promise is a powerful reminder that when God calls us to a mission, He also equips us with His constant presence. Jeremiah's fears of rejection, hostility, and opposition were met with the comforting certainty that he would never be alone. God assured him that He would guide, strengthen, and shield him every step of the way. Such divine support offers encouragement to anyone feeling apprehensive about their calling, highlighting that God's presence is a vital source of strength and courage in uncertain times.

Embracing the Call

Despite his initial uncertainties, Jeremiah ultimately embraced his role as a prophet and dedicated himself to a ministry that lasted over forty years. During this time, he delivered powerful messages of warnings, calls for repentance, and hope to the people of Judah and neighboring nations.

Jeremiah's ministry was not without challenges. He faced immense opposition from those who rejected his messages, often enduring ridicule and hostility from the very people he sought to guide. He also experienced profound personal suffering, including loneliness and despair, especially when met with indifference and rejection.

Despite these trials, Jeremiah remained unwaveringly faithful to God's call. He found strength and assurance in the LORD, believing that his messages were vital for his people's spiritual well-being. Through perseverance and deep faith, Jeremiah continued to proclaim God's truth, demonstrating a remarkable example of commitment and resilience in the face of adversity.

A Reflection for Today

Jeremiah's journey is a powerful example for anyone facing doubts and feelings of inadequacy in their spiritual lives. His story shows that experiencing doubt doesn't mean we are unworthy or incapable of fulfilling God's purposes. Instead, our moments of uncertainty can become valuable opportunities to lean more deeply on God's presence and draw strength from Him.

When we focus on our limitations and weaknesses, we risk missing out on a profound truth: God's power shines brightest when we are at our lowest. Our vulnerabilities allow His strength to come through, showing us that we are not alone in our struggles. This insight encourages us to rethink our perceptions of weakness, recognizing that it's often in our fragile moments that we witness God's greatest work.

Reflecting on Jeremiah's story and the challenges he faced, we find encouragement to embrace our own spiritual journeys with confidence. God equips us with the strength to overcome any obstacles on our path. Our doubts and fears are met with His promise that He will be with us every step of the way, offering guidance, support, and deliverance through even the toughest challenges. With this understanding, we can move forward empowered by faith, knowing that God is always by our side.

CLOSING REMARKS

We may be flawed, but we are also called. Our imperfections do not disqualify us from God's purposes. Instead, they often become the very areas where His power and grace shine the brightest. Throughout this book, we have explored the lives of various biblical figures who, despite their flaws and failures, were chosen by God to fulfill remarkable purposes.

Moses, with his speech impediment, led the Israelites to freedom. David, despite his grievous sins, was a man after God's own heart. Peter, who denied Jesus three times, became the rock upon which the Church was built. Paul, once a persecutor of Christians, became a powerful apostle to the Gentiles. Gideon, who was plagued by fear, delivered Israel from its enemies. Jonah, despite his disobedience, brought repentance to Nineveh. Jeremiah, who doubted his abilities, became a prophet to the nations.

These stories serve as powerful reminders that our weaknesses and imperfections do not diminish our value or potential in God's eyes. On the contrary, they become the very places where His strength and grace are most evident. God's call is grounded in His grace, not our merit. It is an invitation to every believer to embrace the fullness of God's forgiveness and step into the roles He has designed for us, regardless of our past or even our current struggles.

Embrace your calling with confidence, knowing that God equips and empowers the flawed to fulfill His divine mission. Our journey is not about achieving perfection but about responding to God's call with faith and trust. It is about allowing His grace to work through our weaknesses and trusting that He will provide the strength and guidance we need.

Let's step into our calling boldly, for we are flawed but called. May the stories and insights shared in this book inspire you to embrace your imperfections as part of God's beautiful plan for your life. As you move forward, remember that it is not your perfection that qualifies you for God's work but your willingness to respond to His call and trust in His provision.

Together, let us celebrate the incredible ways God uses the flawed to accomplish His remarkable purposes. May you find strength, encouragement, and inspiration in your unique journey, confident that God is with you every step of the way.

SOMETHING TO PONDER

How can you embrace your imperfections and allow God to use them for His greater purpose?

ABOUT THE AUTHOR

Apostle Kevin Riley is the esteemed Founder and Senior Leader of In His Presence Worship Ministries in North Little Rock, AR. His multifaceted roles encompass those of a husband, father, teacher, mentor, psalmist, musician, songwriter, and author. With a life dedicated to leading by example, Apostle Riley inspires others to recognize their identity in Christ and walk in the fullness of their authority.

With over three decades of experience in leadership, teaching, and mentoring, Apostle Riley connects with individuals through a blend of warmth, transparency, and strength. His diverse journey includes serving as a Minister of Music, Sunday School Teacher,

Worship Leader, Worship Pastor, and Lead Pastor. His administrative expertise and Apostolic grace enable him to establish order and guide others to excel in their callings.

A highly sought-after speaker, Apostle Riley has shared his insights at numerous conferences, seminars, and workshops. His mission is to "lead others into the Presence of God and create an atmosphere where the Spirit of God can manifest His undeniable, tangible presence for the ministering, healing, and deliverance of God's people."

In addition to his pastoral duties, Kevin L. Riley is the owner and broker of IHP Real Estate, headquartered in North Little Rock, Arkansas. An award-winning Christian artist, he balances his professional responsibilities with his roles as a dedicated husband, father, and grandfather.

FLAWED BUT CALLED

Kevin's passion for writing has garnered numerous accolades, including awards for his essays, papers, poems, and music. His educational background includes studies at the University of Central Arkansas, Full Sail University, Pulaski Technical College, and Liberty University. A business-minded individual, Kevin seamlessly integrates his entrepreneurial endeavors with his commitment to ministry.

A lifelong reader, Kevin has always cherished the Bible as his favorite book. This deep love for scripture has profoundly influenced his life and ministry. Driven by a passion to help others and impart wisdom through personal experiences, Kevin aims to inspire and uplift those around him.

In his book "Flawed but Called," Kevin conveys the powerful message that imperfections do not disqualify individuals from God's purposes. Instead, they become the areas where His power and grace shine the brightest. Through this work, Kevin encourages readers to embrace their divine calling with confidence, trusting in God's provision and strength.

www.ingramcontent.com/pod-product-compliance
Lightning Source LLC
Chambersburg PA
CBHW071235090426
42736CB00014B/3092